Quantifying the
Value of
Project Management

Quantifying the Value of Project Management

Best Practices for Improving Project Management Processes, Systems, and Competencies

William Ibbs, Ph.D.

Justin Reginato, Ph.D. Candidate

Project Management Institute

Library of Congress Cataloging-in-Publication Data

Ibbs, C. William
      Quantifying the value of project management : best practices for improving project
  management processes, systems, and competencies / William Ibbs, Justin Reginato.
        p.   cm.
      Includes bibliographical references.
      ISBN: 1-880410-96-6
      1. Project management.   2. Project management--Cost effectiveness.   I. Reginato,
  Justin. II. Title.

  HD69.P75 .I233 2002
  658.4'04 – – dc21   2002028714

Design and production of book interior by Project Design Inc.
Design and production of book cover by Kate Pechter.
Editing by Galadriel La Vere.

ISBN: 1-880410-96-6

Published by: Project Management Institute, Inc.
              Four Campus Boulevard
              Newtown Square, Pennsylvania 19073-3299 USA
              Phone: +610-356-4600 or Visit our website: www.pmi.org
              E-mail: pmihq@pmi.org

10   9   8   7   6   5   4   3   2   1

Contents

List of Illustrations

Figures

Tables

Preface

The purpose of this document is to report the results of research by the authors into the quantified benefits of project management. It also can serve as a reference guide on how some organizations are implementing project management processes and practices. It is offered for informational purposes only, and cannot be considered a complete, step-by-step guide to improving your project management function.

Preface

Acknowledgment

This research has benefited from five years of support from many companies, government agencies, non-profit organizations, and people. The Project Management Institute (PMI®) provided seed funding for the research on two separate occasions. Companies that participated in the second research phase of this work include EDS, Northwestern Mutual Insurance Company, Oracle Software Consulting, Procter & Gamble, Prudential Insurance Company, Stamford Health Systems, USAA, and Williams Gas Pipelines. They graciously provided funds, the time of key people, and data from their corporate archives. Support was also received from the University of California at Berkeley. The first phase of the research was reported in *The Benefits of Project Management—Financial and Organizational Rewards to Corporations*, C. W. Ibbs and Young-Hoon Kwak, Project Management Institute, 1997.

Any errors in this report are the sole responsibility of the authors.

Introduction

Project management has become a critical resource for all 21st Century organizations, whether they are for-profit companies, not-for-profit organizations, or government agencies. Yet precious little is known about project management. For example, what project factors lead to successful projects, which project management processes are most important, even what is project success? Speculation and anecdotal experience abound, but little reliable, scientifically-developed, factual information is available to guide senior executives through the project management minefield.

To help answer these and other questions in a more credible and reliable manner, the Project Management Institute (PMI®) provided seed funding for research at the University of California at Berkeley. The result has been a five-year, two-phase research study that has the purpose of quantifying the value of project management.

From this research, three important quantitative findings about project management emerge:

Finding 1: Companies with more mature project management practices have better project performance. For example, companies with more mature practices deliver projects on time and on budget, whereas less mature companies may miss their schedule targets by 40 percent and their cost targets by 20 percent. (See Figures 3-2 and 3-3.)

Finding 2: Project management maturity is strongly correlated with more predictable project management schedule and cost performance. More mature companies, for instance, have a Schedule Performance Index variation of 0.08 and Cost Performance Index variation of 0.11, whereas less mature companies can have corresponding values of 0.16 for both indices.

Finding 3: Good project management companies have lower direct costs than poor project management companies. High maturity companies have project management costs in the 6–7 percent range, while their low maturity counterparts average 11 percent (and in some cases reach 20 percent). Note this percent range is just the cost expended on project management. Organizations with low project management maturity (PMM) jeopardize the likelihood of project success. This impact, in turn, may lead to increased indirect costs, such as late deliveries, missed market opportunities, and dissatisfied customers. The "Project Management Cost Hump" and "The Virtuous Cycle of Project Management" are introduced and discussed in this report; they contend that the ratio of project management costs to project value will actually rise as a company goes from low maturity to somewhat higher maturity. But then that cost ratio will decline as the company reaches higher levels of PMM, principally because it is getting more "project throughput."

These three findings, taken together, are important findings because they are quantitative. They are also important because they prompt other questions that demand further research. For instance:

■ What are the detailed cost components of project management? And is project management success affected more by expenditures on project personnel or systems? This research did develop and apply a cost accounting structure with thirteen components but more details should be captured and analyzed to understand fully how companies spend their project management dollars.

■ What metrics are available to measure parameters such as project scope, customer satisfaction, and quality? This Phase 2 study focused on project cost and schedule, but of course all such performance indicators are interdependent and better methods of measuring project success are needed.

■ How can we better measure the value of project management for internal projects? About one-half of the projects examined in this Phase 2 study were for situations where the project actually has a marketable value; for instance, there is an external relationship between a client who pays a contractor for project services and delivery. Internal projects—for instance, deployment of a new software system developed by and for a company's own personnel—are more difficult to quantify and value. For the purposes of this study we assumed that findings from "external" projects were fairly representative of "internal" projects.

The companies that participated in both studies were promised confidentiality, so there is a limit to how much detail can be reported in this manuscript. Research into the quantified value of project management is an area of ongoing interest to the authors, so these and other, related questions will be the subject of future research. Readers interested in learning more about this continuing work and how their organizations might participate in ongoing studies are invited to contact the authors.

Chapter 1

Project Management Is Increasingly Becoming a Key Corporate Competency

With management models dramatically changing, project management will be forced to follow suit. Increasingly the paradigm for successful businesses is shifting to a loose confederation of business units. Examples of this model include General Electric (conglomerate), BP-Amoco (petroleum and energy), and Johnson & Johnson (pharmaceuticals and medical devices). They are successful because they continually grow revenues and profits and have achieved remarkable stock market capitalization.

These firms share common characteristics such as devolved power, strong emphasis on intellectual property, powerful brand identification, and a premium on project-driven services and products. They are also very much bottom-line focused, managing themselves in a manner that creates increased shareholder value. These companies also share another trait: they are project-focused. As they evolve as organizations, their abilities to deliver projects that advance their corporate strategies also evolve.

To researchers in project management, their most important characteristic is their increasing dependence on projects, making project management a core capability of successful organizations. No longer are being on time and on budget the only benefits or goals of strong project management. Additional core benefits of a project-centric focus and sophisticated project management tools are that they improve upon organizational effectiveness, meeting quality standards, and fulfilling customer satisfaction (Al-Sedairy 1994; Boznak 1988; Bu-Bushait 1989; CII 1990; Deutsch 1991; Gross 1990; Ziomek 1984).

But to be a true core competence, project management success cannot be an occasional event. Performance that is good, on average, is not sufficient. *Repeatable and constant improvement must be the norm.* However, to evaluate the benefits of project management, its value must be quantified. Project management cost, schedule and cost performance, project management maturity, and the return on project management investments (what the authors have termed PM/ROI[SM]) are all important quantifiable metrics in evaluating the benefits of project management. These metrics can help determine whether project management is simply a tool for an organization or a strategic asset.

To fathom the importance of project management, look at just about any industry today. As Figure 1-1 shows, complex, capital-intense projects are in the works everywhere and are becoming more and more prevalent. Before each of these projects received the green light to proceed, extensive financial and market models were used to determine the revenues that may be expected of these multifaceted undertakings. Companies have to evaluate their organizational strengths and weakness prior to initiating these projects. By quantifying their project management capabilities, firms can get a handle on how project management will figure into project success.

Liberal spending for information systems, communications tools, and other complex hardware marked the late 1990s, and project management was an integral part of the spending frenzy. For companies developing software or rebuilding factories, determining product value is relatively easy. Long-established Generally Accepted Accounting Principles (GAAP) will generally allow for a company to determine the

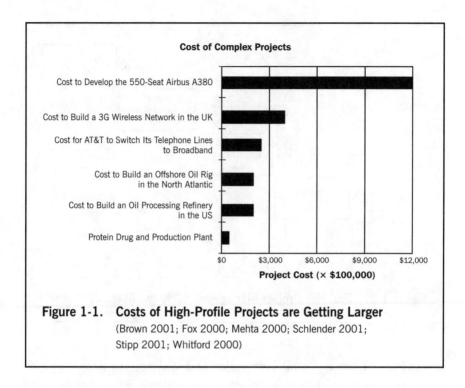

Figure 1-1. Costs of High-Profile Projects are Getting Larger
(Brown 2001; Fox 2000; Mehta 2000; Schlender 2001;
Stipp 2001; Whitford 2000)

financial value of a physical asset with relative ease. It is much more difficult to determine the value of project management services.

How Should We Measure Value?

Price is what you pay. Value is what you get.

Warren Buffett

The question of value depends very much on whose perspective is being taken. Many perspectives exist, such as those of customers, employees, the public-at-large, and so on. Ultimately though, the perspective that matters most is usually that of the owners and investors of the company. A shareholder revolution has occurred within the past decade due to the

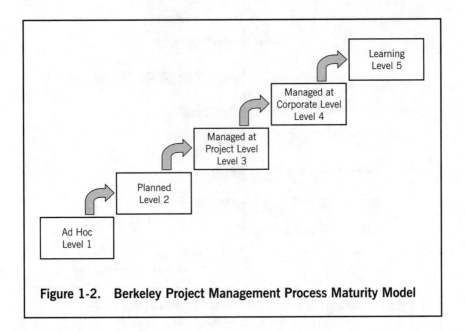

Figure 1-2. Berkeley Project Management Process Maturity Model

emergence of mutual fund companies and widespread pension plans like 401(k)s. Recently, we have seen increasingly fickle shareholders reward profitable companies while bludgeoning others. One Wall Street message is once again clear: *shareholder value is vital.*

Investors are primarily concerned with 1) the return of their capital (profitability); 2) the risk on their capital (safety); and 3) the timing of that return (discounted value). Subpar performance in any one of these three variables must be offset by superior performance in the other two, if it is to be tolerated at all.

What About Project Management?

Project management is about people and the systems, processes, tools, and methodologies they use. Certainly, financial measures alone cannot determine value entirely. As such, determining project management maturity (PMM) is as important as determining the financial payback of project management. One such tool used to determine PMM is the five-

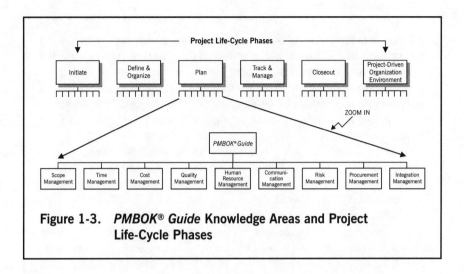

Figure 1-3. ***PMBOK*® *Guide* Knowledge Areas and Project Life-Cycle Phases**

step Berkeley Project Management Process Maturity Model, shown in Figure 1-2. This model demonstrates sequential steps that map an organization's incremental improvement of its project management processes.

The model progresses from nonexistent project management practices to functionally-driven organizational practices to project-driven organizations that incorporate continued project management learning. An organization's position within the model signals its position relative to the other organizations in that industry class or others that have been assessed. The model has been presented in past publications and detailed discussion is included in *Calculating Project Management's Return on Investment* (Ibbs and Kwak 2000).

The Berkley Project Management Process Maturity Model captures both the knowledge areas and project life-cycle phases from *A Guide to the Project Management Body of Knowledge (PMBOK® Guide)* and includes them in the equation when determining PMM. Figure 1-3 displays the *PMBOK® Guide* knowledge areas and project life-cycle phases.

Once PMM is determined and a benchmark for organizational project management drawn, the financial facets can be evaluated.

There have been many methods proposed for determining the financial value of project management. Benefit/Cost analysis is one methodology that has been considered for project management investment

Software A is a producer of enterprise software for small- and medium-sized businesses with $300 million in revenues in 2000. Software B represents the software division of a multibillion-dollar Fortune 500 company. (Both of these companies were studied in Phase 2.) A project management maturity (PMM) assessment was conducted by this research team that revealed how each company's project management practices compared to each other and a composite average of their peers.

The assessment clearly shows that Software A has far superior project management practices than Software B, or even the average for the Software peer group, for that matter. But the global assessment only provides the ends— the means are in the details.

For Software B, simply throwing money blindly at project management is akin to randomly applying bandages to someone who says he feels ill. A PMM assessment pinpoints the source of the project management pain, and in Software B's case major triage is necessary. While lagging behind the peer group in all areas, the categories of quality, risk, planning, and closeout are particularly troublesome, and those areas should be addressed immediately. Because so many categories need attention, Software B may even choose to talk with customers and vendors to help determine which areas of their project management are best to immediately treat.

Conversely, the assessment shows that Software A has the enviable position of besting the peer group in all project management categories, and this gives them several options. They can redirect capital from areas where they are vastly superior to their peers, like procurement, to areas where they have a less surmountable lead, such as cost, especially if members of the value chain appreciate better cost more than superior procurement. Another strategy is to gear product offerings to exploit the areas where Software A excels. For example, Software A scores much higher than the peer group in quality, which also stands as Software B's Achilles' heel. Software A can market their products as high quality, a strategy that peers will find difficult to match and may even bury Software B in such a manner that it may take significant resources and time to recover. Software A may even decide that, while they enjoy the chasm created between themselves and the competition, they have *over*invested in project management and that some money should be redirected to less competitive

Table 1-1.   Mini Case Study: Software Manufacturers

divisions, like development or marketing. By pinpointing project management strengths and weaknesses, the PMM assessment allows companies to accurately and effectively direct capital and resources where they are needed most.

	Software A	Software B	Average for All Software Companies in Phases 1 & 2
Initiate	4.32	2.68	3.35
Define & Organize	4.27	2.68	3.52
Planning	3.72	2.12	3.30
Track & Manage	3.63	2.46	3.32
Closeout	4.21	2.21	3.47
Project-Driven Organization	3.47	2.47	3.02
Communication	4.13	2.40	3.52
Cost	3.45	2.91	3.23
Human Resources	3.50	2.55	3.26
Procurement	4.43	2.57	3.12
Quality	4.08	1.69	3.24
Risk	3.47	2.06	2.87
Scope	4.07	2.50	3.47
Time	3.89	2.39	3.45
Overall Average	3.88	2.39	3.32

Note: Project integration was not assessed for all companies so it was left out of the case. Data reported in the last column of this table were developed from a combination of this Phase 2 study and the Phase 1 study, reported in *The Benefits of Project Management—Financial and Organizational Rewards to Corporations* (Ibbs and Kwak 1997).

Table 1-1. *Continued*

analysis in the past (Knutson 1999). However, it is largely discounted these days because of conceptual flaws, such as the lack of transparency when discounting for the time cost of money and its use in improperly quantifying qualitative measures (Riggs 1984).

Some have suggested balancing tangible and intangible metrics to appraise project management value (Crawford and Pennypacker 2000). They contend that a mix of financial and nonfinancial measures allows companies to track the metrics that matter most to themselves. Unfortunately, in project management settings, such scorecard methods typically deteriorate into mass exercises in measuring for the sake of measuring, with overabundant nonfinancial metrics diluting the effects of the value measurement process (Ittner et al 1997). And even the staunchest scorecard advocates agree that some forms of financial measures (e.g., PM/ROI[SM]) are still needed.

Balanced Scorecard measures are intended to measure the implementation of organizational strategy. Implementation is measured using both qualitative and quantitative measures, yet ultimately coalesces into a capstone financial measure, like Return on Investment (ROI) or Economic Value Added (EVA). The measurement of metrics represents only the means; achievement of strategy is the ends. This distinction is a point often overlooked in recent applications of Balanced Scorecard initiatives (Kaplan and Norton 1996).

Economic Value Added (and corresponding Market Value Added [MVA] for publicly-traded companies) is difficult to apply in a project setting because investments in project management do not always directly and exclusively contribute to a company's market capitalization. EVA determination is a very meticulous procedure, where capital costs must be amortized and pooled costs distributed to the appropriate business unit or project. Also, EVA is dependent on macroeconomic factors, such as the cost of capital, which are not tightly linked to project management effectiveness.

Financial ratios, specifically ROI-based measures, eliminate many of the aforementioned problems. ROI is sharply defined, eliminating the fuzziness introduced into valuation calculations by quantifying nonfinancial measures. As a ratio rather than an absolute number, ROI is also simple to calculate, yet can be expanded to capture cash flows quite simply. With its familiarity to senior executives, ROI is a tractable measure for valuing project management investments.

Accuracy in financial reporting is extremely important in today's information-driven society, and ROI is an accurate measure. Lenders, analysts, and shareholders are constantly vying for steady streams of information. Accurate financial reporting is crucial for companies because their cost of capital is tightly linked to the quality of measurement—the better and more trustworthy the measurement of value, the lower the cost of capital for that organization because of reduced risk to investors. If organizations as a whole use financial ratios like ROI to report the value of the corporation, then project management should follow suit (Tarsala 2001; Ittner et al 1997).

Discussion of PM/ROI[SM]

To fully measure the value of project management, it is desirable to marry the accuracy of a financial ratio like ROI with PMM described above. PM/ROI[SM] combines those two measurements, plus it captures value gleaned from knowledge creation and management, creating one comprehensive project management valuation metric.

Qualitative Value

As stated previously, benchmarking can determine a company's project management effectiveness by capturing qualitative data. The Berkeley Project Management Process Maturity Model captures project management-specific steeped information in *PMBOK® Guide* focus. A second dimension, project life-cycle phases, are also analyzed so that value can be measured as a function of project duration. Qualitative data gleaned from benchmarking can determine the value that policies and procedures add to project management.

Quantitative Value

Quantifiable financial measures can determine project management's monetary value. PM/ROI[SM], along with continuous financial data input, can be used in calculating the cash flow ROI. This subsequently allows for the calculation of the internal rate of return using risk and inflation-adjusted assets, asset life, capitalized operating leases, and so on, and it takes the weighted average cost of capital (WACC) and time-cost of money into effect. While seemingly complex, it can be easily calculated with a spreadsheet and yields the most accurate financial measurement of value (Knight 1998). ROI is then compared to a Minimum Attractive Rate of Return (MARR). If ROI is greater than MARR, the investment is feasible. If it is not greater, the investment probably should not be pursued unless there are compelling nonfinancial motivations.

Return on Investment is also easily translatable across both companies experiencing rapid growth or concentrating on capital or market preservation. Positive movements in ROI can be tracked by rapidly increasing returns (growth companies), and by increasing margins and/or decreasing capital (return companies) (Ferracone and Masuda 2000). However, quantifying the benefits and costs can be tricky. Also, there are always competing requests for investment capital, and a ROI greater than a MARR for project management does not automatically lead to an investment in project management.

Various factors can be used as risk surrogates, and must be treated in a proper analysis. Often risk is handled by adjusting the MARR or WACC in line with the presumed and perceived risk of the investment.

Knowledge Management

The third and final pillar of the strength of PM/ROI[SM] is that it allows organizations to capture the project management value generated from knowledge management. The fifth and highest level of PMM in the Berkeley Project Management Process Maturity Model is based upon sustainable learning. Value creation, more than ever, is correlated with the knowledge-based organization, and the ability to learn translates into the ability to create seemingly insurmountable business advantages (Holland 1994). The Berkeley Project Management Process Maturity Model, as an example, is defined so that organizations with PMMs approaching Level 5 are constantly adding new knowledge to their base of information, resulting in operations that improve themselves over time. The acquisition of knowledge begets new knowledge, all of which leads to super-competitive advantages (Hamel 2000). The knowledge created and used by project management creates an additional lever from which competitive advantage can be exploited.

Chapter 2

Study Methodology

The research detailed in this report is a continuation of the work incubated by the Project Management Institute (PMI®) report entitled *The Benefits of Project Management—Financial and Organizational Rewards to Corporations* (Ibbs and Kwak 1997). Whereas the first report employed a "breadth" approach to assessing companies, canvassing the companies on general tendencies—average project performance or aggregate project management cost—this report takes a "deep" look at the quantifiable data gleaned from the thirty-eight original organizations, as well as fourteen additional organizations. This approach resulted in research that was deeper and yielded data of much higher quality. The result is a Phase 2 study that appears, on the surface, to have fewer data points than the Phase 1 study. But, in truth, this data is more reliable and actually has more depth. As reported in Figure 3-2, for instance, there are twenty-one data points (i.e., companies) but actually sixty-eight projects behind those twenty-one companies.

To ensure strict quality control, each assessed company designated one person who served as the point of contact. This contact was responsible for firm-wide data (such as total cost of project management spending) and was also given the responsibility of collating the disparate project data. Each of the companies or organizations analyzed in this report submitted at least two projects for detailed investigation. Project managers provided information that was used to compute project management maturity (PMM). Additionally, some of the companies listed Key Performance Indicators (KPIs) that they are currently using to gauge project management performance within their respective organizations. The Berkeley researchers, in turn, would spot check by phone or in person those responses as a form of audit.

The project management benchmarking procedure developed and used to assess the project management process maturity in the previous Phase 1 study has been upgraded to accommodate the integration of additional metrics for this new Phase 2 study. This new project management process maturity assessment tool, based upon six project life-cycle phases and nine knowledge areas of *A Guide to the Project Management Body of Knowledge (PMBOK® Guide)*, was employed in this research. A refined version of the five-step Berkeley Project Management Process Maturity Model introduced in the previous Phase 1 study was upgraded in this study.

The collected data measures the relative sophistication and maturity of different organizations and industries. Project management cost, schedule performance, and budget performance data were collected from these organizations for recently completed, representative projects. The previous research has already shown a positive association to exist between a company's PMM and its project cost and schedule performance. In this Phase 2 study, cost and schedule data are analyzed in more detail. For example, project management costs are more clearly delineated. The Phase 2 study also addresses the complication of budget and baseline consistencies between companies (e.g., authorized budget at concept versus authorized budget at contract signing). Additionally, the association between project management cost, as a percentage of total project management costs, and PMM was analyzed.

For the most part, the data in this Phase 2 study were collected from information technology (IT) projects. Some projects were internal (that is, an IT department within Northwestern Mutual developing a software solution for itself). The balance were external (e.g., EDS doing work for one of its clients). Such projects tend to be small in size (say, $1 million and less than one year duration) compared to construction projects, but quite complicated because the underlying scope and technology change rapidly and because such IT is usually being integrated into an existing suite of software products.

The data submitted by Williams Gas Pipeline and Procter and Gamble were for construction projects.

A key assumption for the purposes of this study is that learnings extracted from external projects are applicable to and representative of internal projects. Another key assumption is that the research findings derived from IT projects are relevant to other industries. Of course, it would be prudent to conduct further research to test these assumptions. But because the entire field of project management is founded on the premise that there is great commonality and universality in project management practices across all industries, the authors believe that these are reasonable assumptions.

After the data were collected, each assessment was followed up by a post-mortem interview. These interviews served a dual purpose: they permitted the research team to further probe for more detailed information, as well as provided an opportunity to "spot check" data supplied with the completed assessment tool. The research team was cognitive of the need for data integrity, and steps were taken to ensure such.

The data gleaned in the Phase 2 study were used, in conjunction with data from the past study, to develop curves that show predicted cost, budget, and schedule performance levels for a specific PMM level. We used data from the prior study when their integrity and function were consistent with the goals of this study. The curves are determined by the equations with the highest R^2, or best fit, value. (The statistical curve-fitting function in Microsoft® Excel® offers a choice of curve shapes to be tested: polynomial, exponential, and so on.) These curves can then be used by the individual organization to estimate what project performance gains might reasonably be expected if the organization takes steps to improve its PMM. That information, in turn, can be used to estimate its specific PM/ROI[SM].

Statistical analyses were performed on *all* data available. That is, the Berkeley research team did not exclude any "outliers." Excluding outliers might change the shape and R^2 value of a particular curve fit, but the authors wanted to minimize imposing such judgment into the research.

It is inevitable in a research investigation of real-world business practices that the data would be scattered because of the differences among participating companies, range of projects studied, and other exogenous variables. In actuality, the authors believe that the tendencies and findings of this study are impressively consistent for an empirical study of corporate practices.

At the same time, to be useful to all levels of management, the authors include and report not just quantitative results but also qualitative and anecdotal learnings. For instance, Figure 5-3, the Virtuous Cycle of Project Management, is a concept that is developed from considerable data, yet presented in schematic format for the benefit of readers who are not familiar or interested in highly statistical presentations.

Chapter 3

Companies with More Mature Project Management Practices Have Better Project Performance

Moving the discussion of maturity and value to the next level, the question needs to be asked: What do companies get for their investments in project management? The answer depends in part on how the investments are translated into higher maturity.

Analysis of detailed project management maturity (PMM) assessments reveals that companies with higher PMM tend to deliver projects on time and on budget. Specifically, higher PMM corresponds to increased Schedule Performance Index (SPI) and Cost Performance Index (CPI). SPI and CPI are ratios of total original authorized duration or budget versus total final project duration or cost, respectively, as shown in Figure 3-1.

The value to organizations is apparent. In terms of schedule, as maturity increases so does the ability to complete projects on time. An SPI ratio of 1.00 equates to finishing projects in exactly the time that

$$\text{Cost Performance Index (CPI)} = \frac{\text{Planned Budget}}{\text{Final Costs}}$$

$$\text{Schedule Performance Index (SPI)} = \frac{\text{Planned Duration}}{\text{Final Duration}}$$

Figure 3-1. Equations Determining CPI and SPI

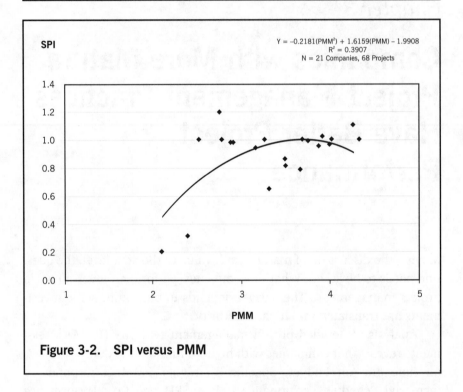

$Y = -0.2181(PMM^2) + 1.6159(PMM) - 1.9908$
$R^2 = 0.3907$
N = 21 Companies, 68 Projects

Figure 3-2. SPI versus PMM

was originally estimated. The ability to accurately forecast the time necessary to complete a project affords senior executives in the firm a powerful tool in meeting time-to-market windows. See Figure 3-2.

Like SPI, CPI also increases with increasing PMM. Also similar to SPI, a CPI value approaching 1.00 signifies accuracy in estimating and delivering project budget. Increasing CPI is good, to a point. The ability

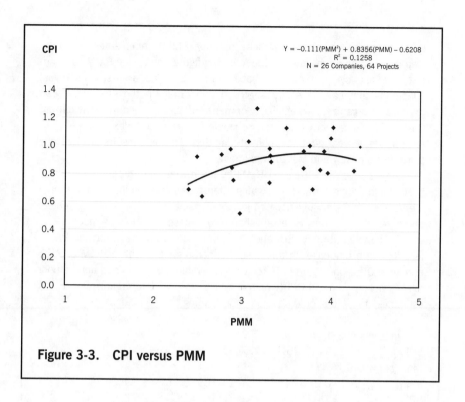

Figure 3-3. CPI versus PMM

to accurately forecast project costs allows companies to confidently allocate capital. See Figure 3-3.

Budgets, more than schedules, tend to be overestimated from the data presented in this study. Based on data revealed by the assessment process, CPI values significantly greater than 1.00 correspond to overly conservative original schedule estimates. If an organization consistently overestimates the time necessary to deliver a project, then its CPI value will be considerable greater than 1.00. *And that can be bad for the company, just like underestimating schedule and budget can be bad.*

An example dealing with this discussion is presented in Table 3-1.

In many cases, project management maturity (PMM) improvement is a two-step process. As represented in the following figure, increasing PMM can consist of efficiency- and maturity-based gains. Detailed assessments reveal conditions that can be easily improved upon that, in the near term, can improve an organization's efficiency of managing projects and move its current Cost Performance Index (CPI) and Schedule Performance Index (SPI) performance in the vertical direction, constituting Step 1. These results are typically gains that are easy and fast to implement.

Step 2 involves increasing PMM by improving upon organizational skill bases for the long term. These gains often mean overcoming organizational inertia and long-standing poor project management habits. A strong project management base must be established before these gains can be made.

To demonstrate how SPI and CPI can be improved by improving PMM, let's look at a real case. In this case, SupplyCo started with a PMM of 3.25 and felt a 0.50-point gain to 3.75 was achievable. SupplyCo had done a poor job of tracking SPI and CPI (which is typical of low PMM organizations), but estimates of how it should have been performing can be made.

In terms of SPI:

$$SPI_{Current} = -0.2181\,(3.25)^2 + 1.6159\,(3.25) - 1.9908$$
$$SPI_{Current} = 0.957$$
$$SPI_{Maturity\ Target} = -0.2181\,(3.75)^2 + 1.6159\,(3.75) - 1.9908$$
$$SPI_{Maturity\ Target} = 1.002$$

This results in an SPI gain of 0.045, or 4.7 percent.

In terms of CPI:

$$CPI_{Current} = 0.244\,(3.25)^2 - 1.632\,(3.25) + 3.6519$$
$$CPI_{Current} = 0.925$$
$$CPI_{Maturity\ Target} = 0.244\,(3.75)^2 - 1.632\,(3.75) + 3.6519$$
$$CPI_{Maturity\ Target} = 0.963$$

This results in a CPI gain of 0.038, or 4.1 percent.

Table 3-1. Mini-Case Study of One Company: Cost and Schedule Performance

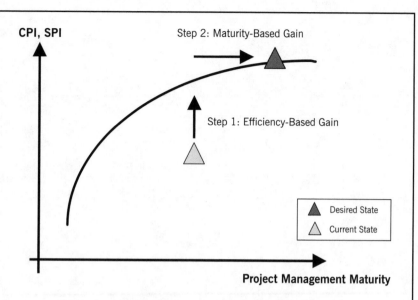

Two-Step Project Management Maturity Improvement

Note: These curves are changing all the time as more data is collected. Do not use these curves for any specific situation without first contacting the authors!

Table 3-1. *Continued*

Chapter 4

Better Project Management Leads to More Reliable Cost and Schedule Performance

Even more important than improving Schedule Performance Index (SPI) and Cost Performance Index (CPI) ratios, companies with higher project management maturity (PMM) deliver projects with more predictable schedule and cost results. As companies improve their PMM, their individual SPI results tend to deviate less from the overall SPI average; see Figure 4-1.

As also seen with these data, CPI standard deviation also decreases as project management skills improve. Companies with high PMM are less likely to have projects where the budgets escalate out of control. Budget accuracy reduces fiduciary risk. For capital-intensive projects, this result can lead to a reduction in the cost of capital and large savings for companies that borrow money for project budgets, or higher financial ratings for companies that obtain project financing from the capital markets. See Figure 4-2 for the CPI standard deviations.

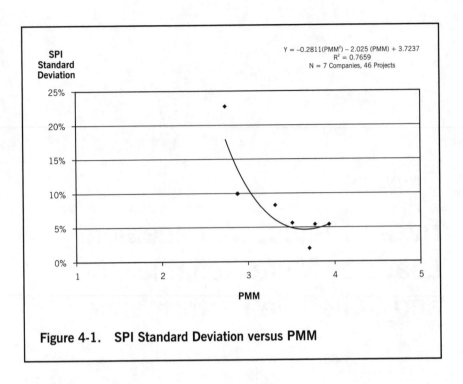

SPI Standard Deviation

$Y = -0.2811(PMM^2) - 2.025\ (PMM) + 3.7237$
$R^2 = 0.7659$
$N = 7$ Companies, 46 Projects

PMM

Figure 4-1.   SPI Standard Deviation versus PMM

Having an *average* SPI or CPI of 1.00 means that the final project duration is equal to the originally estimated project duration. A subtle point that many people overlook is the *reliability* of SPI and CPI metrics. Many people think that an SPI or CPI that averages less than 1.00 is good, whereas in truth this is not necessarily the case. It is of little help to that company in estimating project durations if half of its projects have an SPI of 1.25 and the other half 0.75. The variation thwarts effective planning and management of multiple projects. Similarly, a company that has an average SPI and CPI substantially under 1.00 is being too conservative in its estimates. It may be "leaving money on the table" and not undertaking as many projects as it could with more realistic forecasts.

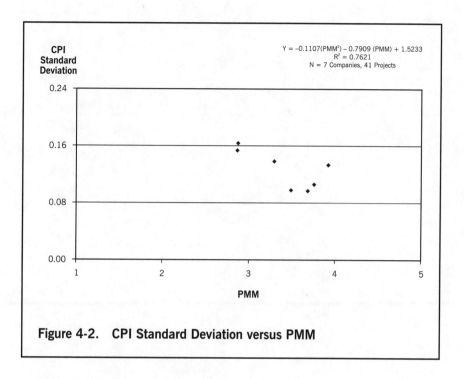

Figure 4-2. CPI Standard Deviation versus PMM

Consider for instance a company that budgets a number of projects at the outset of a year. It then proceeds to finish those projects at a better-than-estimated rate, say SPI = 0.92. Of course this means that it performs 8 percent better than planned. But it also means that the company has some underutilized resources over the course of the year.

Figures 4-1 and 4-2 are built on the experiences of a relatively few number of companies, seven and seven respectively, but a large number of projects, forty-six and forty-one, which, in statistical terms, means there is a reliable number of degrees of freedom.

Chapter 5

Good Project Management Can Cost Less

The title of this section is good news to both project managers and senior executives. The only problem is that companies often have to expend a lot of effort and resources to create a great project management practice. By segregating companies by project management maturity (PMM) and the percentage of project costs consumed by project management, clear trends come to light.

As the trend line in Figure 5-1 displays, the project management cost ratio increases as PMM increases until PMM reaches approximately Level 3. From there the project management cost ratio steadily decreases with increasing PMM. This signifies that investments in project management are necessary to establish a functional level of PMM (approximately PMM = 3.00). However, once that level of PMM is achieved, the costs necessary to maintain it decrease as a firm's project management competency improves.

What does this mean? For companies investing in project management, hoping to move from low maturity to high, the costs involved in the investment will initially outstrip the benefits. Yet eventually, the

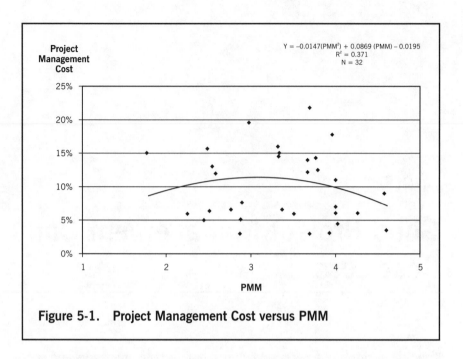

Figure 5-1. Project Management Cost versus PMM

investments pay off, as mature companies actually pay less, as a percentage of project management costs, to improve their PMM, as depicted in Figure 5-2.

Figure 5-2, not drawn to scale, approximates the trends in project management cost and PM/ROI[SM] as companies improve their PMM. Typically, Zone I companies have low PMM and spend little on project management. This situation inherently makes sense, since companies that spend little money could be expected to have a low PMM. Typically, companies that have assessed their project management skills, but fall in this category of low PMM, have established an initiative to improve project management processes. These companies have established a baseline for growth. The diagram definitions are based on in-depth observations at five companies that submitted a total of forty projects. The lines are approximations or conceptualizations formed by observations of quantitative data. The lines were adjusted to "fit" the rest of the observations made by the authors.

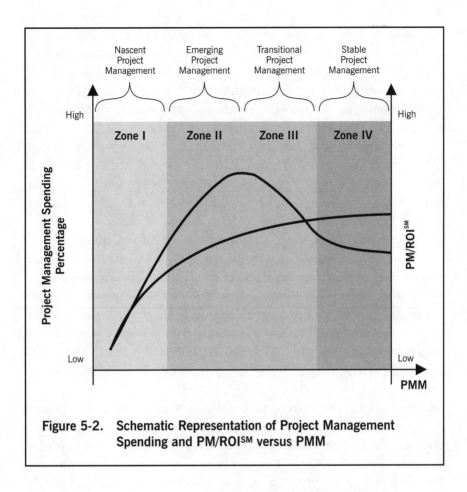

Figure 5-2. Schematic Representation of Project Management Spending and PM/ROI^{SM} versus PMM

To improve overall PMM, most organizations will elect to invest capital in improving people, processes, and tools. As an organization moves from Zone I to Zone II, its PMM increases, as does its PM/ROI^{SM}. As project management starts to improve past an ad hoc assemblage of skills, PMM begins to emerge. However, these improvements do not come cheap—project management cost starts increasing as well and at a steeper pace.

Once an organization reaches Zone III, it has achieved a PMM and PM/ROI^{SM} superior to most companies. The gains in PMM remain relatively expensive, but the company has "gotten over the project management investment hump." The company may actually be spending more on project management, but it is getting more project throughput so its unit costs are lowered. It is important not only to maximize returns on project management but to minimize the cost of project management as well. Money not spent on project management can be invested in a company's core business.

Organizations that have reached Zone IV have arrived at "project management nirvana." Not only is PMM maximized, but it is done so at a lower project management cost percentage than other peer companies. In Zone IV, the spread between PM/ROI^{SM} and project management cost widens favorably for the organization.

From observations made with the previous Phase 1 study data and in-depth interviews with many of the companies assessed in both phases, the authors have been able to create the following effectiveness matrix that displays *The Virtuous Cycle of Project Management*, shown in Figure 5-3. Similar to the Boston Consulting Group's matrix for determining business viability, The Virtuous Cycle of Project Management matrix allows organizations to map their PMM and investments in project management to ensure they are progressing in a logical and sustainable manner.

The axes of the matrix display PM/ROI^{SM} and project management cost percentage against one another. This diagram is based on observations at twenty-four companies. Quadrants were divided so that each was represented by an equal number of companies. The boundary between "good" and "bad" project management cost percentage (the vertical axis) is approximately 5 percent to 7 percent; the PM/ROI^{SM} division is approximately 26 percent to 30 percent. Because PM/ROI^{SM} and PMM are tightly linked, substantial gains in PMM and in PM/ROI^{SM} can be achieved as an organization moves from left to right along the x-axis. Project management growth normally goes through the clockwise cycle depicted on this diagram.

Companies in the lower left-hand quadrant are underinvested in project management and are earning low returns, if any. Without adequate investment, both PMM and PM/ROI^{SM} will continue to lag behind peer organizations.

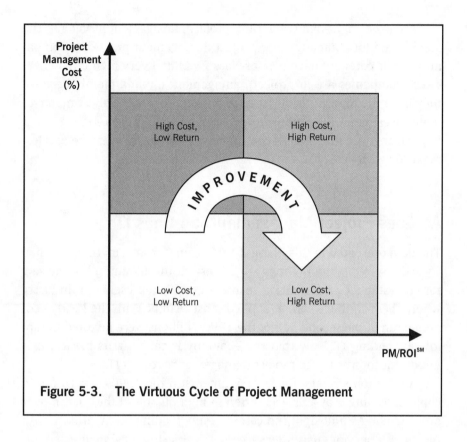

Figure 5-3. The Virtuous Cycle of Project Management

Continuing to the upper left-hand quadrant is the next logical place to progress, but it is an area where no organization should reside for any prolonged duration. In this quadrant, project management investments have begun to increase, but benefits have not yet been fully realized. Organizations whose project management practices exist in this region for extended periods are vastly underperforming their peers.

In the upper right-hand quadrant, the benefits of improving project management are starting to be realized within the organization, but the cost of those improvements is still steep. While having a high PM/ROI^SM is commendable, it is a somewhat Pyrrhic victory in that project management is still costly for these companies. And, the additional capital could be reinvested in the project itself.

The lower right-hand quadrant, project management nirvana, is the ideal locale for company-wide project management practices. Companies in this category have best-of-class PMM and very high PM/ROI[SM]. These companies are in project management nirvana mainly because they have the highest throughput of projects for their project management investment. For organizations in this arena, project management is a strong organizational competence and, even in some circles, regarded with awe.

As Goes Project Management, So Goes IT

The data presented in this Phase 2 study comes from a myriad of industry sectors. While the findings are consistent throughout all of the sectors investigated, information technology (IT) represents an industry where these findings can be applied most readily. With the heady economic run of the second half of the 1990s, billions were invested in rapidly expanding IT. Now that the economy is catching its breath, it is important to investigate project management's role in IT.

A common strategy for IT assignments in the 1990s was to throw copious resources at a project, often in high pursuit of the "first mover advantage." As hindsight indicates, simply loading an IT project with resources does not guarantee success. IT project management is no different. More important than escalating project management resources, it is necessary to find the "sweet spot" where resources correspond to effectiveness. In other words, spending more on IT project management does not ensure success.

For the technology companies and projects studied by the authors, all confirmed the conclusions made thus far. Even more interesting, these findings mirror a 1997 study made by McKinsey and Company regarding IT. In that report it was found that many firms investing in IT were finding themselves climbing a slippery slope. Despite heavy investments in technology, little in the way of financial benefits was being reaped. Technology portfolios were unwieldy, and complexity had left organizations frustrated and overburdened. Companies that found themselves in this position were located in an area referred to as the "IT

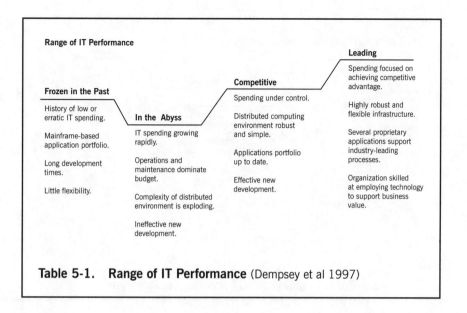

Range of IT Performance

Frozen in the Past

History of low or erratic IT spending.

Mainframe-based application portfolio.

Long development times.

Little flexibility.

In the Abyss

IT spending growing rapidly.

Operations and maintenance dominate budget.

Complexity of distributed environment is exploding.

Ineffective new development.

Competitive

Spending under control.

Distributed computing environment robust and simple.

Applications portfolio up to date.

Effective new development.

Leading

Spending focused on achieving competitive advantage.

Highly robust and flexible infrastructure.

Several proprietary applications support industry-leading processes.

Organization skilled at employing technology to support business value.

Table 5-1. Range of IT Performance (Dempsey et al 1997)

abyss." Companies that had successfully avoided or navigated the abyss had IT portfolios that made them competitive of leading companies (Dempsey et al 1997). Table 5-1 shows the range of IT performance.

A similar abyss exists for project management. The project management abyss is akin to being located in the upper left-hand quadrant of The Virtuous Cycle of Project Management matrix. In the abyss, organizations contribute generous amounts of resources without receiving reciprocating benefits. While these characteristics apply to all types of projects, they are particularly prevalent in the IT realm. Furthermore, they confirm the viability of The Virtuous Cycle of Project Management matrix. Understanding the quantifiable value of project management is vital to avoiding similar investment chasms.

Building on the McKinsey model, IT project management can be viewed as having a range of performances. As displayed in Table 5-2, organizations on the far left of the performance spectrum tend to have project management practices that are not lending themselves to organizational performance. While spending in project management remains a low priority, IT spending is not. These organizations have low PMM and their ability to implement solutions reflects that.

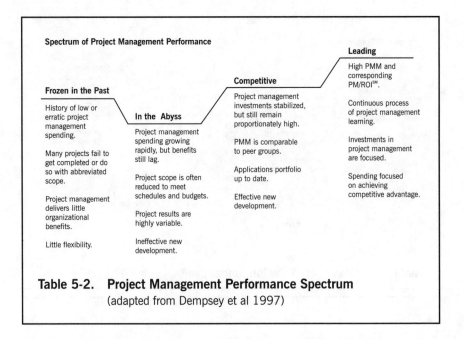

Spectrum of Project Management Performance

Leading

High PMM and corresponding PM/ROI℠.

Competitive

Frozen in the Past

Project management investments stabilized, but still remain proportionately high.

Continuous process of project management learning.

History of low or erratic project management spending.

In the Abyss

PMM is comparable to peer groups.

Investments in project management are focused.

Many projects fail to get completed or do so with abbreviated scope.

Project management spending growing rapidly, but benefits still lag.

Applications portfolio up to date.

Spending focused on achieving competitive advantage.

Project management delivers little organizational benefits.

Project scope is often reduced to meet schedules and budgets.

Effective new development.

Project results are highly variable.

Little flexibility.

Ineffective new development.

Table 5-2.   Project Management Performance Spectrum
(adapted from Dempsey et al 1997)

Realizing that little investment in project management is not bearing any fruit in terms of implementing IT, many organizations move dangerously close or into the project management abyss. As IT spending increases, so does project management spending. However, without clearly pinpointing the appropriate areas to invest, many of those investments fail to reach the space in which they are needed. Not realizing where they're at, organizational managers start to throw good money after bad, creating a never-ending vortex of poor IT project management investments.

For organizations that have focused project management goals, incremental investments tend to solve localized problems, and PMM grows accordingly. This outcome demonstrates the importance of benchmarking—without having a starting point, investments in project management are difficult to apply. Still, after spending large sums of capital while treading water in the abyss, and more still to get out, arriving at competitive levels of project management is still costly.

Three large diversified financial companies spent considerable amounts of money on information technology (IT) in 2000, of which Customer Relationship Management (CRM) and database software constituted a large percentage. Consider the data in the following table.

The data clearly show that Financial X has the highest IT costs per employee of the peer group. After a detailed interview, it was revealed that Financial X has difficulty completing projects, particularly large, complex database assignments. The inability to fulfill project requirements either within budget or with a complete scope is represented by their low project management maturity (PMM). It is also of no surprise that they spend the least on project management of the peer group.

Financial Z, on the other hand, is in an exactly opposite position—they have a relatively high PMM and are able to complete projects on time and within budget while spending considerably less than Financial X on IT on the whole. However, they spend a whopping 21.8 percent of project budgets on project management. Financial Z is, in essence, *over*spending its way to good project management practices. While enjoying stronger IT assets and a higher PM/ROI[SM] than its peers, the assessment process has helped Financial Z in understanding that they need to get better throughput of the capital invested in project management. Financial Z is in the process of implementing a plan to reduce project management spending while maintaining its high PMM, allowing it to reduce capital expenditures and maintain its best-of-class status.

Financial Y is in the middle, in terms of project management competency. While being average from a project management standpoint, they spend considerably less than most of their peers, escaping the modestly increasing returns of overinvestment demonstrated by Financial Z. However, Financial Y's adequate investment in project management allows them to sidestep the inadequacies that result from lack of investment and maturity, as is suffered by Financial X. Considering that project management is not a core competency for any of these companies and they derive no actual revenue from it, Financial Y appears to have optimized its project management investment and practice, while still spending, by far, the least on IT per employee. It has found the project management "sweet spot."

Table 5-3.   Mini-Case Study: Software Application

In both of these cases, there is more information beneath each of these situations. However, the use of PMM and PM/ROI[SM] are demonstrated in a manner that displays how such information can be readily used by an organization to assess its project management practices.

	Financial X	Financial Y	Financial Z
IT Spending per Employee[1]	$43,900	$16,600	$36,400
Project Management Maturity	2.90	3.49	3.69
Project Management as a Percentage of Project Costs	5.2%	7.0%[2]	21.8%
PM/ROI[SM]	21%	26%	27%

[1] (Riley, Laiken, and Williams 2001)

[2] Figure represents a qualitative judgment; detailed project costs were not collected.

Table 5-3. *Continued*

For companies that can make it to the far right of The Project Management Performance Spectrum, project management is a tool for creating business value. Investments in project management are focused and have immediate impact. Most important, since organizations in this position have high PMM, the cost of maintaining robust practices requires smaller investments. In this region, PM/ROI[SM] is maximized. The data collected throughout this Phase 2 study also provides commentary to the fact that organizations that make it to the far right of Table 5-2 have lower Schedule Performance Index and Cost Performance Index variability. It can therefore be concluded that quantifying project management's benefits and measuring project success march together in lock step.

Table 5-3 looks at a mini-case study involving software application.

Chapter 6

Success of Projects Is Often Judged by the Processes They Incubate

In many cases, if not most, processes are born of successful projects. As such, many companies determine project success as a function of processes they create. This is particularly accurate in industrial, manufacturing, and construction settings.

Typically listed as Key Performance Indicators (KPIs), these metrics were based on several factors. For organizations engaged in information technology (IT) projects, these metrics typically involved personnel utilization rates. Many companies implementing large software and hardware conversions tracked personnel utilization because of the large amount of consultants involved. Utilization rates are usually expressed in terms of how much it costs in total to employ a single person per hour. By combining utilization data against schedule and cost metrics, a company can determine whether it is easier to use internal staff or consultants. Tracking this information is extremely important to determining the cost of project management and subsequent value.

Many companies building industrial production plants and facilities tracked measures such as:

■ Operating System Reliability: Ratio of total run time versus total run time available.

■ Manufacturing Cost to Operate: Ratio of manufacturing cost delivered versus manufacturing cost promised.

■ Production Rate: Ratio of rate delivered to rate promised.

While these metrics may appear independent of project management metrics like Schedule Performance Index (SPI), Cost Performance Index (CPI), and project management cost, they are very much related to project management maturity (PMM). More and more, process plants are required to do more with less. That is, production must have maximum throughput in order to minimize costs. Throughput is a function of facility quality. Not only do facilities need to be delivered on time to ensure timely product delivery, but plants and equipment must meet exact specifications to ensure that they will run under taxing production cycles.

One large personal consumable product company observed by the authors was in a recent cycle of reducing the number of total factories worldwide in an effort to reduce costs. The products it sells can be defined accurately as commodities—they are often differentiated from other products only by price—although this company operates as a premium brand. Despite shutting almost twenty facilities (an average facility can cost in the hundreds of millions of dollars) in the past ten years, this company has been able to improve its production rate (defined as rate delivered/rate promised) from 50 percent to over 95 percent. In that same ten-year period, its operating system reliability (defined as production time "running"/total available run time) has also increased from 50 percent to 95 percent, while its cost of manufacturing has remained constant. These improvements have moved lock step with improvements in PMM.

In the past five years, the same company has improved both its SPI and CPI from 0.85 to 0.95. During that same period, PMM improved from 3.69 to 3.92. While the improvements in PMM cannot be directly related to the productivity improvements because they cover differing periods (the past five years versus the past ten), they certainly lend

In addition to the improvements in manufacturing or process productivity that can be gained from superior project management practices, the benefits from being on time are also obviously quite substantial. To illustrate, let's look at ManufactureCo. Due to the functional nature of ManufactureCo's products, we were able to estimate the early revenue that will be generated from its projects in terms of 2001 dollars. Exact figures are not included to maintain ManufactureCo's anonymity. The following calculations are intended to demonstrate the value of projects to ManufactureCo, from which one can then infer the value in lost revenue due to late delivery of such projects.

ManufactureCo collected $40 in 2000, which represents $40 per year in revenue.

ManufactureCo has $22.6 in buildings and equipment (ManufactureCo's Project Management Department is charged with constructing buildings, plants, and equipment). However, the $22.6 value of buildings and equipment represents its worth over its amortized lifetime. Therefore, a yearly value of buildings and equipment must be calculated.

	Buildings	Equipment
Percent of Projects	35%	65%
Amortization Period*	20 years	10 years

*The amortization periods were estimated from industry practices. ManufactureCo is in the process of aggressively amortizing buildings and equipment to get them off of its balance sheet.

Therefore, the blended lifespan of buildings and equipment at ManufactureCo is:

$$(10 \text{ years})(65\%) + (20 \text{ years})(35\%) = 13.5 \text{ years}$$

Therefore, the one-year value of buildings and equipment at ManufactureCo is:

$$\$22.6/13.5 \text{ years} = \$1.67$$

Table 6-1.   Mini-Case Study: Additional Value Calculations

credible evidence to the link between improved PMM and manufacturing excellence. In fact, representatives of that company openly state that their project management department must constantly push the

So, if ManufactureCo earned $40 for one year with buildings and equipment worth $1.67 for one year, then ManufactureCo realizes:

$$(\$40)/(\$1.67) = \$23.95$$

That is, $23.95 in revenue per year is earned for every $1 of buildings and equipment.

In 2000, ManufactureCo spent $2.8 on buildings and equipment. That $2.8 will have an average yearly worth of:

$$(\$2.8)/(13.5 \text{ year}), \text{ or } \$0.207 \text{ yearly}$$

The value, in terms of 2000 dollars, will be:

$$(\$0.207)(\$23.95) = \$4.97$$

Therefore, the $2.8 spent in 2000 on buildings and equipment will result in $4.97 in yearly revenue. Put another way, projects have approximately 77.5 percent yearly return on investment.

From this calculation, one can postulate that failure to complete projects on time will result in the missed opportunity for large amounts of revenue. It should be noted that production is not solely dependent on new projects being completed—production can be shifted to other facilities or equipment can be operated at a higher capacity than usual—but significant revenue is dependent on project completion.

Table 6-1. *Continued*

limits of their skills to help the company as a whole maintain their position as an industry leader. They estimate that project management is partially responsible for $150 to $200 million a year in facility cost savings.

In Table 6-1 a mini-case study depicting additional value calculations is presented.

Chapter 7

Concluding Remarks and Next Steps

Project management has value. That has been clearly shown in this research. While the overwhelming majority of practitioners agree with that statement, prior claims have not been substantiated by academic research. At best, these claims have been "supported" by questionable, anecdotal information. By quantifying the value of project management with this more rigorous and objective study, its benefits become clear and translatable across a multitude of platforms and languages.

Defining project management's value requires a combination of qualitative and quantitative metrics. Most importantly, the value must be presented in quantifiable terms. This can be achieved by combining measures of project management maturity (PMM) with a financial measure like PM/ROI^{SM}. This research has displayed that as PMM increases, so does PM/ROI^{SM}. Besides increasing PM/ROI^{SM}, mature organizations enjoy superior schedule and cost performance. Even more important, increased PMM is linked with reduced standard deviations of Schedule Performance Index (SPI) and Cost Performance Index (CPI). This result means that as organizations become more mature, the variability in their projects is reduced, leading to repeatable project success. Repeatability is a key component of core competency, and the most mature project management practices lend themselves as organizational competencies to companies.

Quantifying project management has the additional benefit of classifying project management effectiveness. Not only can project management investments be expressed in terms of value, but also they can help categorize project management and help track benefits as investments increase and practices mature. Understanding project management in terms of maturity, PM/ROI^{SM}, and project management cost can be a valuable tool in sidestepping project management investment pitfalls, delivering organizations from the abyss of throwing large investments after mediocre results.

Despite all the improvements in quantifying project management's value presented throughout this publication, more work needs to be done. In particular, further research is necessary for quantifying the benefits of project management associated with internal projects. Without the ability to determine the market value of internal projects, project management is, in turn, also difficult to value. Models that show project management's contribution to corporate success and profitability are desperately needed.

The collection of data for project management valuation also needs improvement. While the authors have succeeded in creating a cost collection form that assembles broad and deep project management costs, better tools must be further developed. Data delineating between personnel and systems must be collected to ensure that project management investments are being made in the most appropriate places.

Data regarding metrics such as project scope, customer satisfaction, and quality must also be collected with greater lucidity and precision. While the natural response to, and prevailing practice of, measuring these fields is to use qualitative metrics, value can only be accurately derived via quantitative metrics. Our research is currently focusing on developing quantitative measures to better understand the questions that have already been raised in this report and undoubtedly will be raised during future research investigations.

References

Al-Sedairy, Salman T. 1994. Project Management Practices in Public Sector Construction: Saudi Arabia. *Project Management Journal* (December): 37–44.

Boznak, Rudolph G. 1988. Project Management—Today's Solution For Complex Project Engineering. *IEEE Proceedings*.

Brown, Stuart F. 2001. How To Build A Really, Really, Really Big Plane. *Fortune* (March 5): 146.

Bu-Bushait, K. A. 1989. The Application of Project Management Techniques to Construction and R&D Projects. *Project Management Journal* (June): 17–22.

Construction Industry Institute. 1990. Assessment of Owner Project Management Practices and Performance. *Special CII Publication* (April).

Crawford, Kent, and James Pennypacker. 2000. *The Value of Project Management: Why Every 21st Century Company Must Have an Effective Project Management Culture*. Center for Business Practices.

Dempsey, Jed, Robert E. Dvorak, Endre Holen, David Mark, and William F. Meehan. 1997. Escaping the IT Abyss. *The McKinsey Quarterly* 4: 80–91.

Deutsch, Michael S. 1991, November. An Exploratory Analysis Relating the Software Project Management Process to Project Success. *IEEE Transactions on Engineering Management* 38(4).

Ferracone, Robin, and Bertha Masuda. 2000. It's the New Economy: Who Said Anything About Returns? *World at Work* (Fourth Quarter): 55–60.

Fox, Justin. 2000. A Piece of the Action. *Fortune* (October 9): 141.

Gross, Robert L., and David Price. 1990. Common Project Management Problems and How They Can be Avoided through the Use of Self Managing Teams. *1990 IEEE International Engineering Management Conference*.

Hamel, Gary. 2000. *Leading the Revolution*. Boston, MA: Harvard Business School Press.

Holland, Robert C. 1994. Summary of the Opening Remarks at the Panel on Leadership Development and Organizational Change. *Annual Conference of the World Future Society* (July 24–26): 1–5.

Ibbs, C. W., and Young-Hoon Kwak. 1997. *The Benefits of Project Management—Financial and Organizational Rewards to Corporations*. Upper Darby, PA: Project Management Institute.

———. 2000, June. Calculating Project Management's Return on Investment. *Project Management Journal* 31(2): 38–47.

Ittner, Christopher D., David F. Larcker, and Marshal W. Meyer. 1997. *Performance, Compensation and the Balanced Scorecard*. Philadelphia, PA: The Wharton School—University of Pennsylvania.

Kaplan, Robert, and David Norton. 1996. *The Balanced Scorecard: Translating Strategy into Action*. Boston, MA: Harvard Business School Press.

Knight, James. 1998. *Value Based Management*. New York: McGraw-Hill.

Knutson, Joan. 1999. A 3-part series in *PM Network* (January, February, and July).

Mehta, Stephanie. 2000. The ,000,000,000,000 Bet. *Fortune* (October 9): 128.

Project Management Institute (PMI®) Standards Committee. 1996. *A Guide to the Project Management Body of Knowledge* (*PMBOK® Guide*). Upper Darby, PA: Project Management Institute.

Riggs, James. 1984. *Decision Analysis for Engineers*. New York: McGraw-Hill.

Riley, Michael, Scott Laiken, and John Williams. 2001. *Digital Business Design in Financial Services*. Mercer Management Consulting. White Paper accessed at www.mercermc.com (October 24).

Schlender, Brent. 2001. Microsoft: The Beast is Back. *Fortune* (June 11): 76.

Stipp, David. 2001. Bill Haseltine. *Fortune* (June 25): 112.

Tarsala, Mike. 2001. Making the Most of the Market. *CBS Marketwatch* (May 9).

Whitford, David. 2000. Steel, Sweat, and Oil. *Fortune* (October 2): 202.

Ziomek, N. L., and G. R. Meneghin. 1984. Training—A Key Element in Implementing Project Management. *Project Management Journal* (August): 76–83.

Author Contact Information

Name: William Ibbs, Ph.D.
Title: Professor of Civil Engineering
Affiliations: University of California & The Ibbs Consulting Group
Mailing Address: 1603 Portland Avenue, Berkeley CA 94707 USA
Phone: +510-558-3475
Email: DRCWIbbs@aol.com

Name: Justin Reginato, MS
Title: Graduate Researcher
Affiliations: University of California, Berkeley
Mailing Address: 555 Pierce Street #1520C, Albany, CA 94706 USA
Phone: +510-289-0407
Email: jregi@uclink.berkeley.edu

Upgrade Your Project Management Knowledge with Leading Titles from PMI

A Guide to the Project Management Body of Knowledge (PMBOK® Guide) – 2000 Edition

Project Management Institute

The Project Management Institute's (PMI®) *PMBOK® Guide* has become the essential sourcebook for the project management profession and its de facto global standard, with over 900,000 copies in circulation worldwide. It has been designated an American National Standard by the American National Standards Institute (ANSI) and is one of the major references used by candidates to study for the Project Management Professional (PMP®) Certification Examination. This new edition incorporates numerous recommendations and changes to the 1996 edition, including: progressive elaboration is given more emphasis; the role of the project office is acknowledged; the treatment of earned value is expanded in three chapters; the linkage between organizational strategy and project management is strengthened throughout; and the chapter on risk management has been rewritten with six processes instead of four. Newly added processes, tools, and techniques are aligned with the five project management processes and nine knowledge areas.

ISBN: 1880410230 (paperback)
ISBN: 1880410222 (hardcover)
ISBN: 1880410257 (CD-ROM)

The Frontiers of Project Management Research

Dennis P. Slevin, Ph.D., David I. Cleland, Ph.D., Jeffrey K. Pinto, Ph.D., Editors

Tips from cutting-edge research that you can use now! Although humans have been managing projects for thousands of years, from roads and pyramids to the International Space Station, the organization of the activity into a profession has only evolved within the last 50 years. Formal research into the knowledge areas and processes required for successful projects is even more recent, having begun in the early 1960s. This first-of-its-kind publication from the Project Management Institute (PMI®) brings together 28 research papers from internationally known and well-established researchers in project management from around the globe. From them you will glean an insightful overview of past and current research findings, and take an eye-opening excursion along frontiers fertile for future investigation. You will also find a wealth of practical information that you can use now in managing your projects, be they organizing meetings, producing new products, or building skyscrapers.

ISBN: 1880410745 (hardcover)

The Certified Associate in Project Management (CAPM™) Role Delineation Study

Project Management Institute

This helpful book can answer many of your CAPM™ questions—and more! As project management grows in scope, importance, and recognition, so do the related career options. Here, straight from The Project Management Institute (PMI®) is a look is a look at the latest important global certification. The Certified Associate in Project Management (CAPM) certification lends professional credibility to men and women as they start their project management career path. This work tells the story of the development of the CAPM examination and outlines the knowledge a practitioner must master in order to pass the examination. Further, it offers a glimpse into the activities and responsibilities of CAPMs in the workplace. *The Certified Associate in Project Management (CAPM) Role Delineation Study* should be required reading for anyone who wants to pursue this certification.

ISBN: 1880410982 (paperback)

Project Manager Competency Development Framework

Project Management Institute

Sharpen your project manager skills now! Discover the career benefits of climbing into the Project Management Institute's (PMI®) new competency development framework. Like an evolving building's transparent superstructure, the competency framework enables you to clearly see the interdependencies between your job knowledge, skills, and behavior. Readily uncover areas of outmoded or faulty construction and tackle only what needs renovating. Enjoy the clarity! Researched by senior-level PMI members for four years, The *Project Manager Competency Development Framework* has the primary purpose of sharpening the skills of project management practitioners everywhere. It also guides the professional development of aspiring project management practitioners. Organizations will find the framework useful in guiding practitioners to their fullest potential. Individuals will find the framework useful in guiding the development of their own project management competence against a recognized standard.

ISBN: 1880410974 (paperback)

PM 102 According to the Olde Curmudgeon

Francis M. Webster Jr.

In this eagerly awaited follow-up to *PM 101*, Francis M. Webster Jr., a.k.a. the Olde Curmudgeon, offers a fascinating and very readable guide to getting your project right the first time. Among other issues, he discusses four aspects of quality in projects, the intricacies of risk management, and sixteen ways to reduce project duration. *PM 102* is sprinkled with real-life examples and keen observations born of the author' forty-plus years in the project management field. Four subjects make this book unique. The discussion of the full range of resources available to you includes materials management and the effective use of executives and staffs of your organization. The clear distinction between the project and the product of the project provide a sharper focus on managing aspects of each. The discussion of quality provides a practical framework for minimizing "scope creep." The pragmatic discussion of reporting and control presents tested ways of ensuring that you know what is happening on your project, maintaining urgency throughout the project, and completing the project for a satisfied client.

ISBN: 1880410788 (paperback)

Proceedings of PMI Research Conference 2002

Project Management Institute

The Project Management Institute (PMI®) Research Conference 2002, Frontiers of Project Management Research and Application, co-chaired by Dennis P. Slevin, Ph.D., Jeffrey K. Pinto, Ph.D., and David I. Cleland, Ph.D., held 14–17 July in Seattle, Washington USA, brought together top researchers and practitioners in the project management field. Their purpose was to discuss new learning, ideas, and practices, as well as answer questions in areas that may still need more work. This publication brings their research to your fingertips. The evolution of any profession depends on the breadth and depth of its research. The baselines must be established and then tested. Ideas must grow and change to remain up-to-date with current issues and business practices in the world.

ISBN: 1880410990 (paperback)

Quantifying the Value of Project Management

C. William Ibbs, Ph.D. and Justin Reginato

William Ibbs, Ph.D. and Justin Reginato, from the University of California at Berkeley, explore real-world data from 52 U.S. corporations and find the key to a high return on investment. It is project management maturity. Mature PM departments have more on-time, under-budget projects; less variable schedules and expenses; and decreased cost ratios. Project management maturity benefits extend to the parent company where Dr. Ibbs finds lower utilization rates, higher production rates and lower operating costs. Dr. Ibbs shows how to assess PM maturity and track its development.

ISBN: 1880410966 (paperback)

Project Management Institute Practice Standard for Work Breakdown Structures

Project Management Institute

PMI's first practice standard to complement and elaborate on *A Guide to the Project Management Body of Knowledge (PMBOK® Guide)* – 2000 Edition, this new manual provides guidance and universal principles for the initial generation, subsequent development, and application of the Work Breakdown Structure (WBS). It introduces the WBS and its characteristics, discusses the benefits of using a WBS, and demonstrates how to build a WBS and determine its sufficiency for subsequent planning and control. A unique feature is the inclusion of 11 industry-specific examples that illustrate how to build a WBS, ranging from Process Improvement and Software Design to Refinery Turnaround and Service Industry Outsourcing.

ISBN: 1880410818 (paperback)

The PMI Project Management Fact Book
Second Edition

Project Management Institute

First published in 1999, this newly enlarged and updated "almanac" provides a single, accessible reference volume on global project management and the Project Management Institute (PMI®). Topics include the history, size, explosive growth, and the future of the project management profession; parameters of the typical project; a statistical profile of the individuals working in project management based on recent, global research; the organizational settings in which project management activities take place; and valuable information about the world's largest professional association serving project management, the Project Management Institute. Appendices offer an additional wealth of information: lists of universities with degree programs in project management and PMI Registered Educational Providers; PMI's Ethical Standards; professional awards; a glossary; and an extensive bibliography. This is the central reference for those working in project management and a career guide for those interested in entering the profession.

ISBN: 1880410737 (paperback)

People in Projects

Project Management Institute

Project management is fortunate in possessing a rich and growing body of tools and metrics that aid in helping us to more effectively run our projects. However, that is just what they are: tools and metrics. Project management is no less prone than any other discipline to the problems inherent in managing people. *In fact, a strong argument could be made that project management offers far more people problems than other forms of corporate activity* because it can involve so many levels of tasks, deadlines, cost pressures, the need to accomplish work through teams, and the well-known challenge of helping employees who have great technical skills also develop their people skills. This important book, *People in Projects,* focuses on one of the nine knowledge areas of *A Guide to the Project Management Body of Knowledge (PMBOK® Guide)* – 2000 Edition: human resource management. It is a collection of some of the most important writing relating to the people side of project management that the Project Management Institute has produced in the last six years.

ISBN: 1880410729 (paperback)

Project Management for the Technical Professional

Michael Singer Dobson

Dobson, project management expert, popular seminar leader, and personality theorist, understands "promotion grief." He counsels those who prefer logical relationships to people skills and shows technical professionals how to successfully make the transition into management. This is a witty, supportive management primer for any "techie" invited to hop on the first rung of the corporate ladder. It includes self-assessment exercises; a skillful translation of general management theory and practice into tools, techniques, and systems that technical professionals will understand and accept; helpful "how to do it" sidebars; and action plans. It's also an insightful guide for those who manage technical professionals.

"The exercises and case studies featured here, along with the hands-on advice, hammer home fundamental principles. An intriguing complement to more traditional IT management guides, this is suitable for all libraries." —Library Journal

ISBN: 1880410761 (paperback)

The Project Surgeon: A Troubleshooter's Guide to Business Crisis Management

Boris Hornjak

A veteran of business recovery, project turnarounds and crisis prevention, Hornjak shares his "lessons learned" in this best practice primer for operational managers. He writes with a dual purpose—first for the practical manager thrust into a crisis situation with a mission to turn things around, make tough decisions under fire, address problems when they occur, and prevent them from happening again. Then his emphasis turns to crisis prevention, so you can free your best and brightest to focus on opportunities, instead of on troubleshooting problems, and ultimately break the failure/recovery cycle.

ISBN: 1880410753 (paperback)

Risk and Decision Analysis in Projects
Second Edition

John R. Schuyler

Schuyler, a consultant in project risk and economic decision analysis, helps project management professionals improve their decision-making skills and integrate them into daily problem solving. In this heavily illustrated second edition, he explains and demystifies key concepts and techniques, including expected value, optimal decision policy, decision trees, the value of information, Monte Carlo simulation, probabilistic techniques, modeling techniques, judgments and biases, utility and multi-criteria decisions, and stochastic variance.

ISBN: 1880410281 (paperback)

Earned Value Project Management
Second Edition

Quentin W. Fleming and Joel M. Koppelman

Now a classic treatment of the subject, this second edition updates this straightforward presentation of earned value as a useful method to measure actual project performance against planned costs and schedules throughout a project's life cycle. The authors describe the earned value concept in a simple manner so that it can be applied to any project, of any size, and in any industry.

ISBN: 1880410273 (paperback)

Project Management Experience and Knowledge Self-Assessment Manual

Project Management Institute

Based on the Project Management Professional (PMP®) Role Delineation Study, this manual is designed to help individuals assess how proficiently they could complete a wide range of essential project management activities based on their current levels of knowledge and experience. Included are exercises and lists of suggested activities for readers to use in improving their performance in those areas they assessed as needing further training.

ISBN: 1880410249 (spiral paperback)

Project Management Professional (PMP) Role Delineation Study

Project Management Institute

In 1999, the Project Management Institute (PMI®) completed a role delineation study for the Project Management Professional (PMP®) Certification Examination. In addition to being used to establish the test specifications for the examination, the study describes the tasks (competencies) PMPs perform and the project management knowledge and skills PMPs use to complete each task. Each of the study's tasks is linked to a performance domain (e.g., planning the project). Each task has three components to it: what the task is, why the task is performed, and how the task is completed. The *Project Management Professional Role Delineation Study* is an excellent resource for educators, trainers, administrators, practitioners, and individuals interested in pursuing PMP certification.

ISBN: 188041029X (spiral paperback)

PM 101 According to the Olde Curmudgeon

Francis M. Webster Jr.

Former editor-in-chief for PMI®, Francis M. Webster Jr. refers to himself as "the Olde Curmudgeon." The author, who has spent thirty years practicing, consulting on, writing about, and teaching project management, dispenses insider information to novice project managers with a friendly, arm-around-the-shoulder approach. He provides a history and description of all the components of modern project management; discusses the technical, administrative, and leadership skills needed by project managers; and details the basic knowledge and processes of project management, from scope management to work breakdown structure to project network diagrams. An excellent introduction for those interested in the profession themselves or in training others who are.

ISBN: 1880410559 (paperback)

The Project Sponsor Guide

Neil Love and Joan Brant-Love

This practical guide is intended for executives and middle managers who will be, or are, sponsors of a project, particularly cross-functional projects. It is also helpful reading for facilitators and project leaders.

ISBN: 188041015X (paperback)

Don't Park Your Brain Outside: A Practical Guide to Improving Shareholder Value with Smart Management

Francis T. Hartman

Hartman has assembled a cohesive and balanced approach to highly effective project management. It is deceptively simple. Called SMART™, this new approach is Strategically Managed, Aligned, Regenerative, and Transitional. It is based on research and best practices, tempered by hard-won experience. SMART has saved significant time and money on the hundreds of large and small, simple and complex projects on which it has been tested.

ISBN: 1880410486 (hardcover)

The EnterPrize Organization: Organizing Software Projects for Accountability and Success

Neal Whitten

Neal Whitten is a twenty-three-year veteran of IBM and now president of his own consulting firm. Here he provides a practical guide to addressing a serious problem that has plagued the software industry since its beginning: how to effectively organize software projects to significantly increase their success rate. He proposes the "Enterprize Organization" as a model that takes advantage of the strengths of the functional organization, projectized organization, and matrix organization, while reducing or eliminating their weaknesses. The book collects the experiences and wisdom of thousands of people and hundreds of projects, and reduces lessons learned to a simple format that can be applied immediately to your projects.

ISBN: 1880410796 (paperback)

Teaming for Quality

H. David Shuster

Shuster believes most attempts at corporate cultural change die because people fail to realize how addicted they are to the way things are, the root causes of their resistance to change, and the degree to which their willingness to change depends on the moral philosophy of management. His new book offers a stimulating synthesis of classical philosophy, metaphysics, behavioral science, management theory and processes, and two decades of personal teaming experience to explain how individuals can choose change for themselves. Its philosophy-to-practice approach will help people team in ways that promote exceptionally high levels of bonding, individual creative expression (innovation), and collective agreement (consensus). Shuster shows how personal work fulfillment and corporate goals can work in alignment.

ISBN: 188041063X (paperback)

Project Management for Managers

Mihály Görög and Nigel J. Smith

Everything in *Project Management for Managers* revolves around getting an organization to the future it wants for itself. From start to finish, these topics are examined and analyzed, and eventually understood and appreciated. Practical realities are integrated into the authors' philosophies, not ignored or reduced to mere methods and techniques. Görög and Smith place developing the right organizational structure, risk management methodology, contracts, and cost estimates into a unified context. *Project Management for Managers* is the book every project manager needs. It adds context and understanding to the methods and techniques we crave.

ISBN: 1880410540 (paperback)

The Juggler's Guide to Managing Multiple Projects

Michael S. Dobson

This comprehensive book introduces and explains task-oriented, independent, and interdependent levels of project portfolios. It says that you must first have a strong foundation in time management and priority setting, then introduces the concept of Portfolio Management to timeline multiple projects, determine their resource requirements, and handle emergencies.

ISBN: 1880410656 (paperback)

Recipes for Project Success

Al DeLucia and Jackie DeLucia

This book is destined to become "the" reference book for beginning project managers, particularly those who like to cook! Practical, logically developed project management concepts are offered in easily understood terms in a lighthearted manner. They are applied to the everyday task of cooking—from simple, single dishes, such as homemade tomato sauce for pasta, made from the bottom up, to increasingly complex dishes or meals for groups that in turn require an understanding of more complex project management terms and techniques. The transition between cooking and project management discussions is smooth, and tidbits of information provided with the recipes are interesting and humorous.

ISBN: 1880410583 (paperback)

Tools and Tips for Today's Project Manager

Ralph L. Kliem and Irwin S. Ludin

This guidebook is valuable for understanding project management and performing to quality standards. Includes project management concepts and terms— old and new—that are not only defined but also are explained in much greater detail than you would find in a typical glossary.

ISBN: 1880410613 (paperback)

The Future of Project Management

Project Management Institute

Developed by the 1998 PMI® Research Program Team and the futurist consultant firm of Coates and Jarratt, Inc., this guide to the future describes one hundred national and global trends and their implications for project management, both as a recognized profession and as a general management tool. It covers everything from knowbots, nanotechnology, and disintermediation to changing demography, information technology, social values, design, and markets.

ISBN: 1880410710 (paperback)

Book Ordering Information

Phone: +412.741.6206
Fax: +412.741.0609
Email: pmiorders@abdintl.com
Mail: PMI Publications Fulfillment Center
PO Box 1020
Sewickley, Pennsylvania 15143-1020 USA

Visit PMI's website at www.pmi.org
